Score

Unlimited Praise 1
10 Sacred Ensemble Arrangements

For any combination of instruments

CURNOW®
M U S I C

EXCLUSIVELY DISTRIBUTED BY

HAL•LEONARD®
CORPORATION

7777 W. BLUEMOUND RD. P.O. BOX 13819 MILWAUKEE, WI 53213

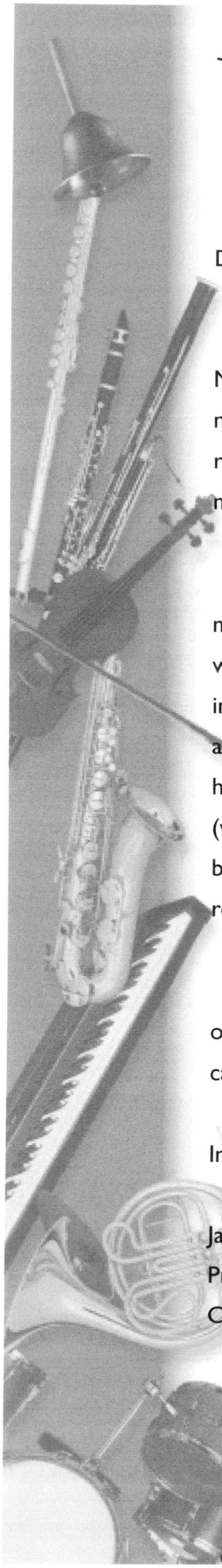

Unlimited Praise 1

Dear Friends,

Please allow me this opportunity to introduce the first edition of Curnow Music Press new flexible sacred ensemble series for use with your church, community or school small, medium or large ensemble. Over the past few years I have received many requests for music to fill this very important area of instrumental music, so I hope that you will take time to look through these materials.

UNLIMITED PRAISE was designed with the sacred ensemble conductor in mind. Arranged by internationally known composers/arrangers, these ten pieces will work well with every instrumental ensemble imaginable, including quartets of mixed instruments, praise bands, full band or orchestra, and brass band. The arrangements are designed to be playable by an average grade 3 (strong middle school or average high school) player. Each arrangement includes optional descant (fifth part), keyboard (with chords included for use with guitar), percussion (mostly drum set) and electric bass parts. These parts enhance the overall sound of the arrangement, but are not required for performance. This gives the conductor unlimited ways to use the series.

My prayer, and the prayers of the arrangers, is that you will be able use any or all of these pieces in whatever type of worship and praise service you may be called upon to participate, and that your praise will always be, Unlimited Praise.

In Christ,

James Curnow
President
Curnow Music Press, Inc.

Order number: CMP 0517.01

UNLIMITED PRAISE 1
Score
iSBN 90-431-1190-2

Table Of Contents

Page

How to use Unlimited Praise

As long as there is one player on each of the four main parts, these arrangements will work. In fact, if you have only one or two instrumentalists and play Part 1 and 2, along with the piano (and possibly bass and drums), these arrangements will still be extremely effective. After each of those four parts is covered, it is up to the conductor to decide how the other instruments will be used (see chart below for instrumentation possibilities). The possibilities are unlimited. Once instrumentation is established, the conductor of larger ensembles can choose to have just woodwinds, brass or strings play specific sections in order to provide variety in timbre. Another possibility would be to select any of the four main parts to be played by just woodwinds, brass, or strings.

Available books

PART NAME	INSTRUMENTATION	EDITION NUMBER
Descant C	Flute, Oboe, Bells, Violin	0551.01 CMP
Descant B♭	B♭ Clarinet, B♭ Trumpet	
Part 1 C	Flute, Oboe, Bells, Violin	0552.01 CMP
Part 1 B♭	B♭ Clarinet, B♭ Trumpet	0553.01 CMP
Part 1 E♭	E♭ Alto Saxophone, E♭ Trumpet/Cornet, E♭ Clarinet	0554.01 CMP
Part 2 C	Violin	0555.01 CMP
Part 2 B♭	B♭ Clarinet, B♭ Trumpet	0556.01 CMP
Part 2 F	F Horn, English Horn	0557.01 CMP
Part 2 E♭	E♭ Alto Saxophone, E♭ Alto Horn	0558.01 CMP
Part 3 B.C.	Bassoon, Trombone, Euphonium, Cello	0559.01 CMP
Part 3 𝄡	Viola	0560.01 CMP
Part 3 B♭	B♭ Tenor Saxophone, B♭ Euphonium T.C.	0561.01 CMP
Part 3 F	F Horn	0562.01 CMP
Part 3 E♭	E♭ Alto Clarinet, E♭ Alto Saxophone, E♭ Alto Horn	0563.01 CMP
Part 4 B.C.	Bassoon, Trombone, Euphonium, Tuba, Cello, Double Bass	0564.01 CMP
Part 4 B♭ T.C.	B♭ Bass Clarinet, B♭ Contra Bass Clarinet, B♭ Euphonium T.C., B♭ Bass T.C.	0565.01 CMP
Part 4 E♭ T.C.	E♭ Contralto Clarinet, E♭ Baritone Saxophone, E♭ Bass T.C.	0566.01 CMP
Keyboard	Piano, Synthesizer, Organ (Guitar Chords included)	0567.01 CMP
Percussion	Drum Set	0568.01 CMP
Electric Bass	Electric Bass, Double Bass	0569.01 CMP
Score		0517.01 CMP

1. HE IS LORD

Duration: 2:20

Arr. **James Curnow** (ASCAP)

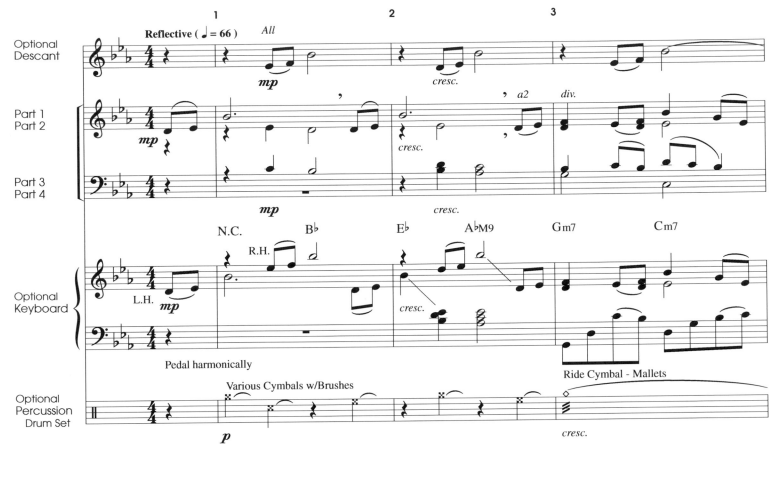

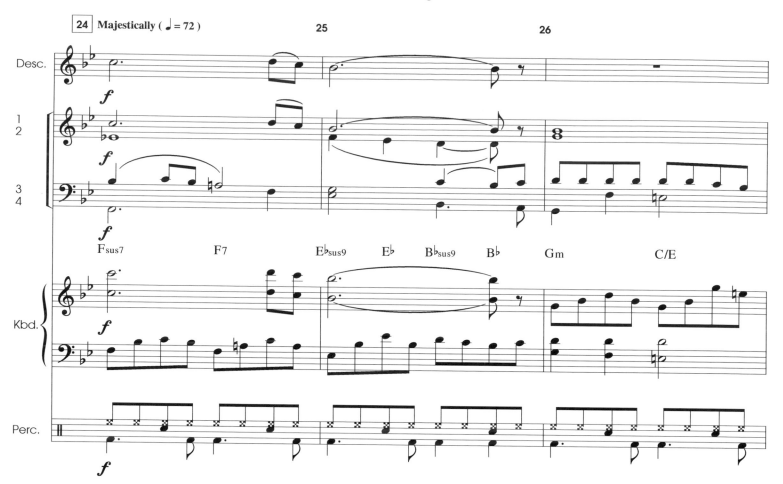

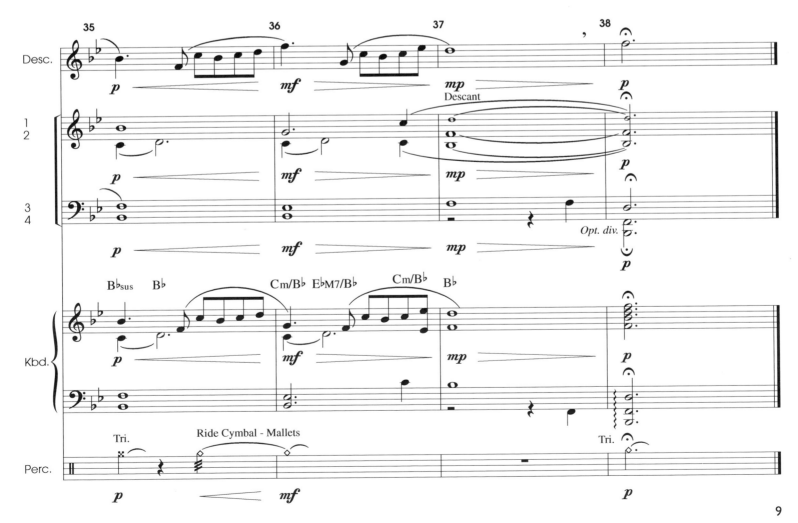

Duration: 2:00

2. ALL HAIL THE POWER
Coronation

Arr. **Timothy Johnson** (ASCAP)

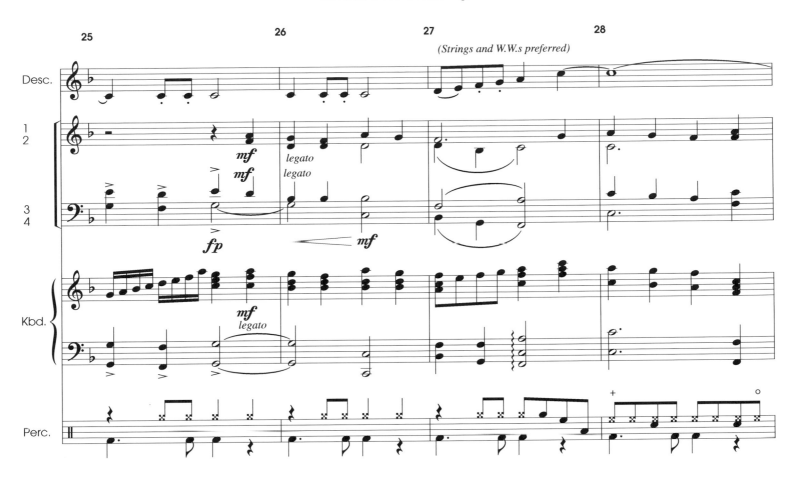

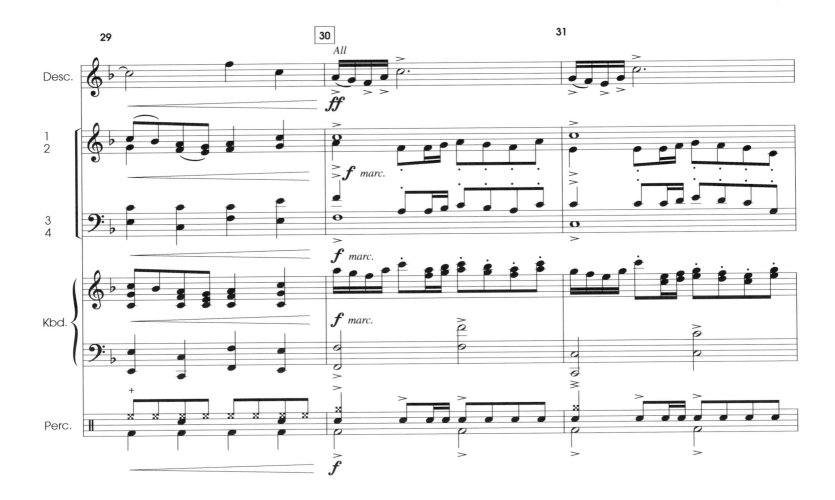

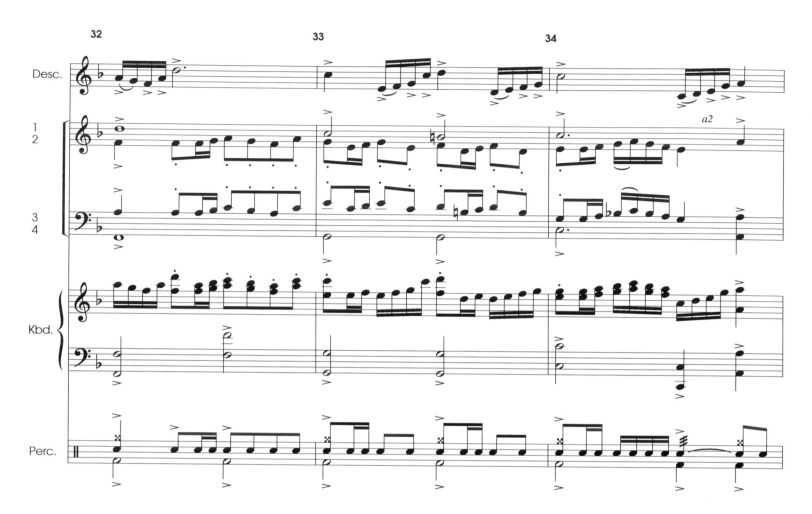

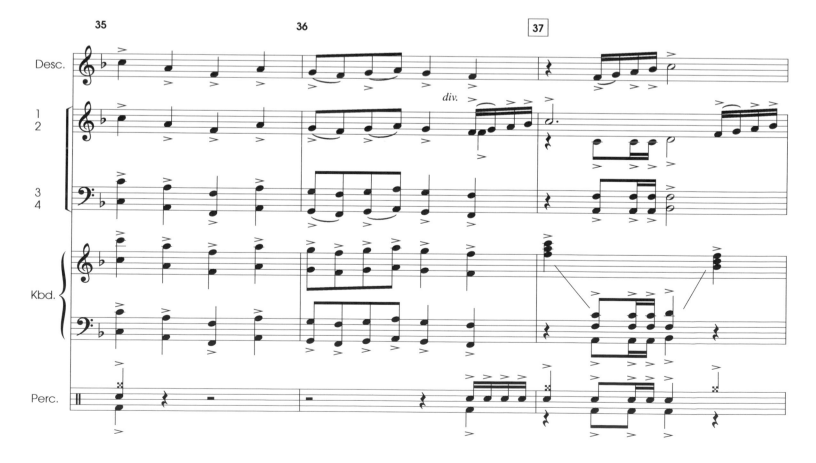

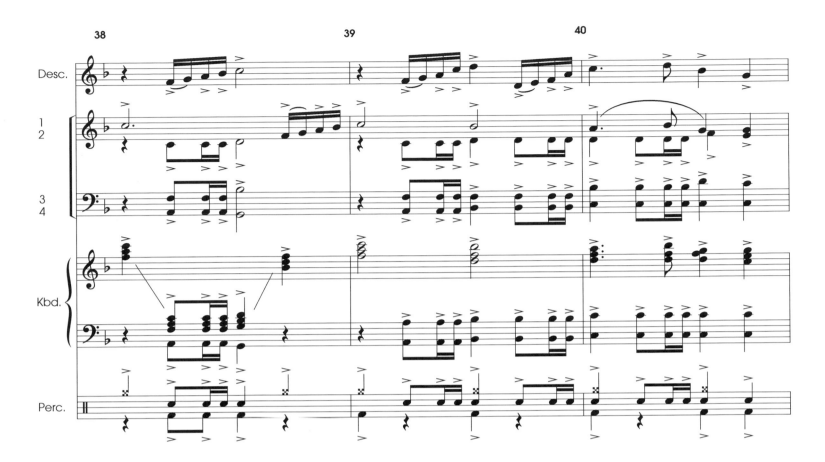

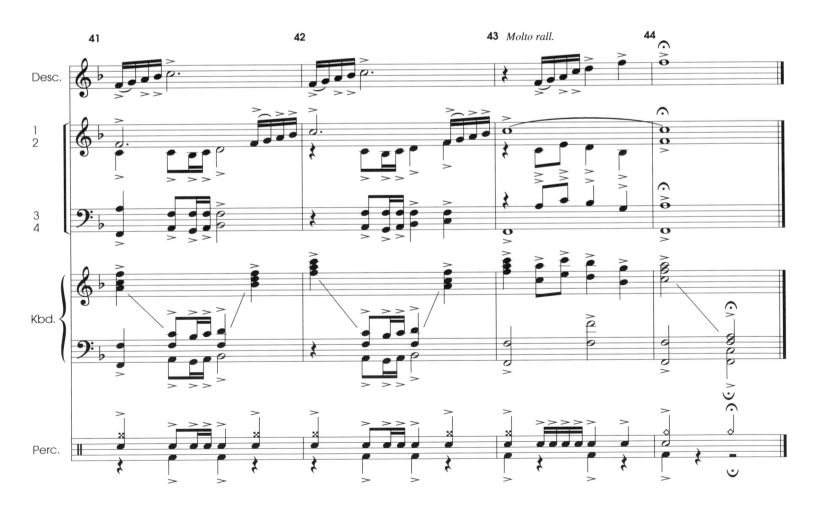

3. WHAT A MIGHTY GOD WE SERVE

Duration: 1:45

Arr. **Douglas Court** (ASCAP)

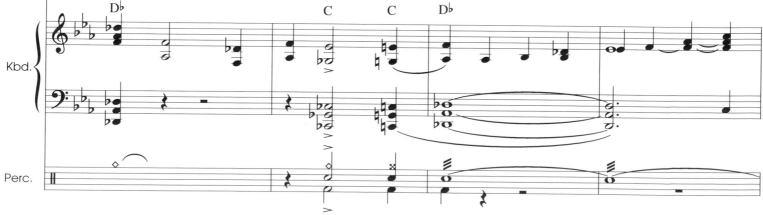

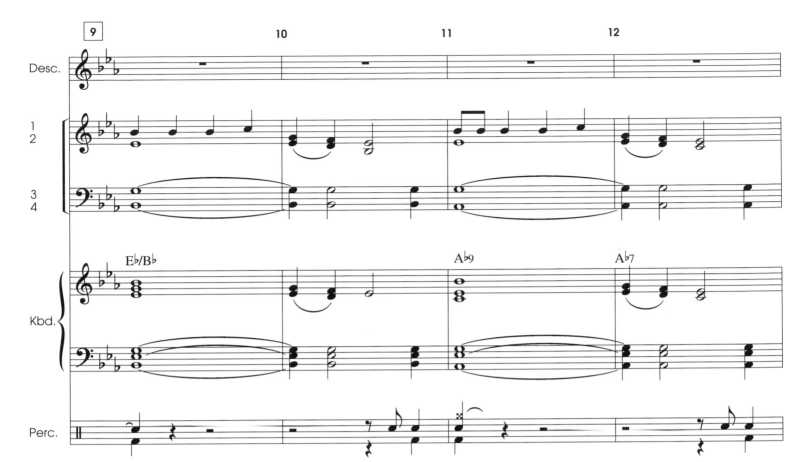

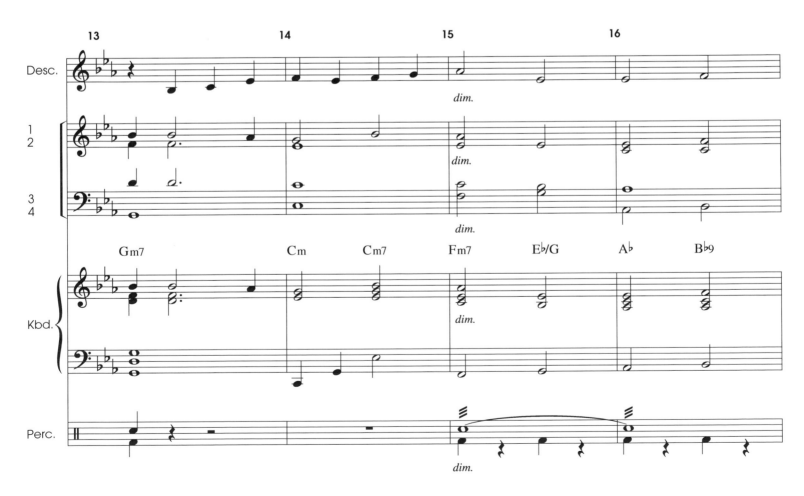

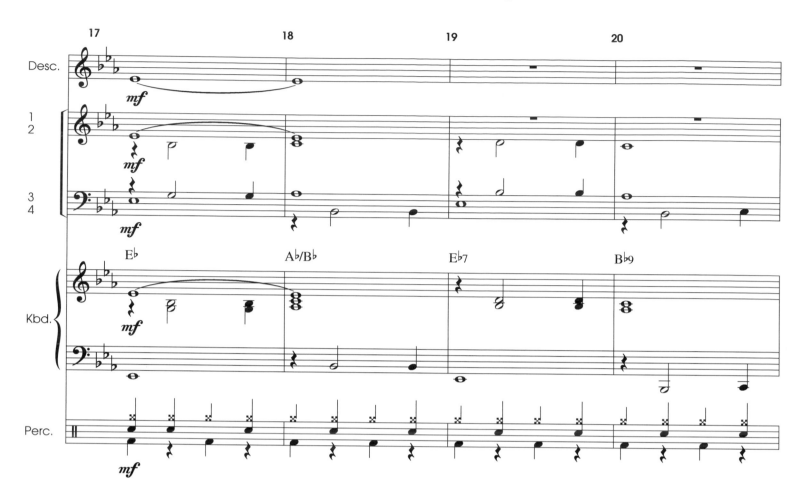

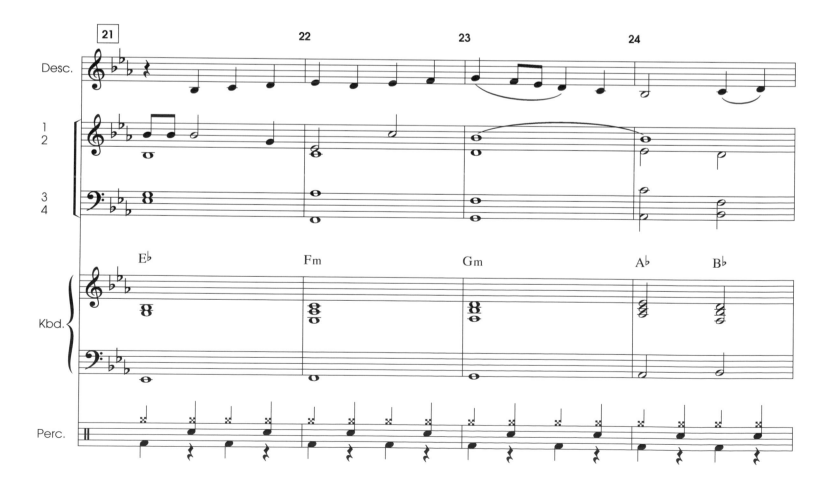

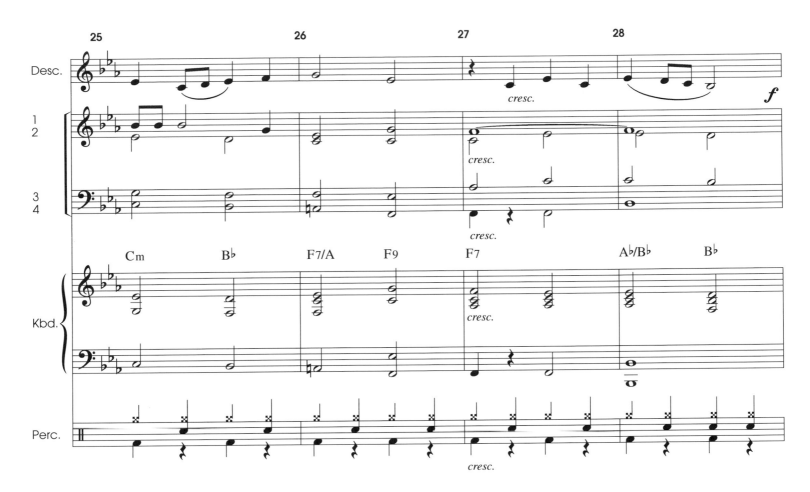

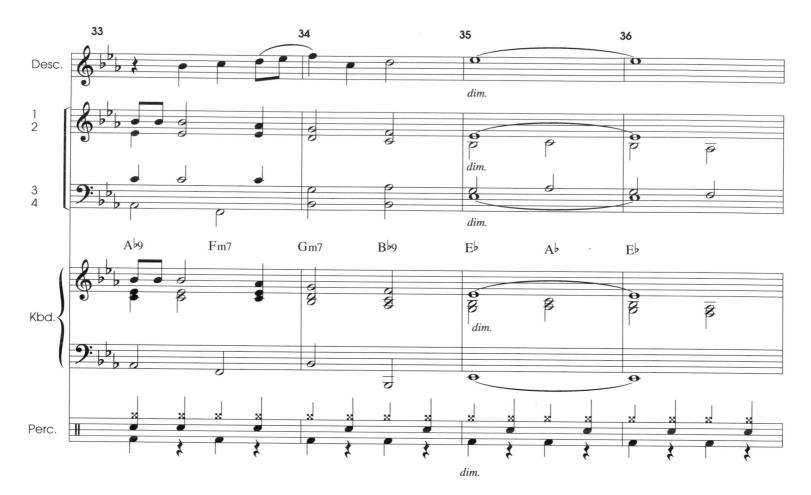

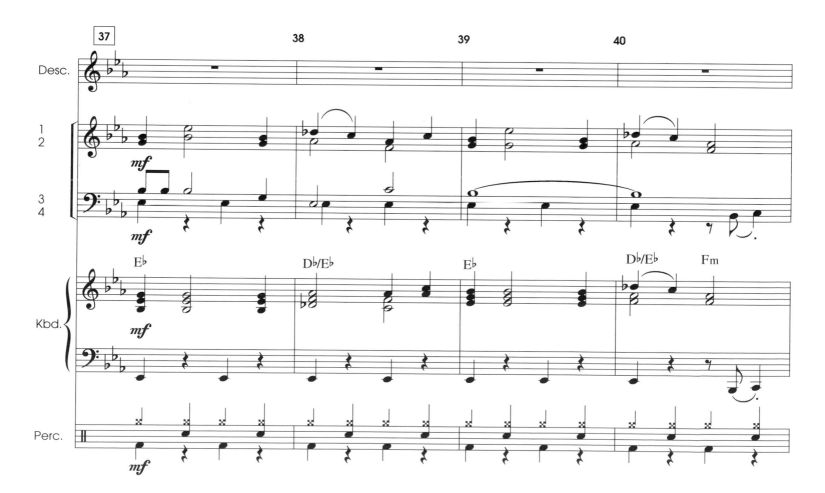

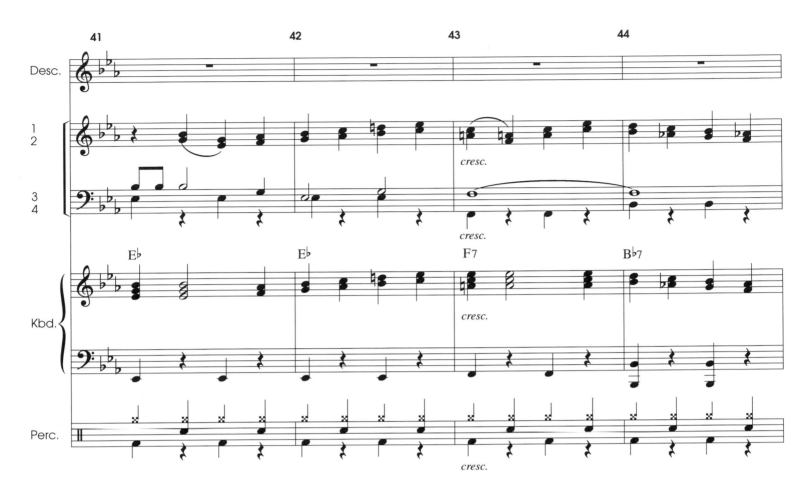

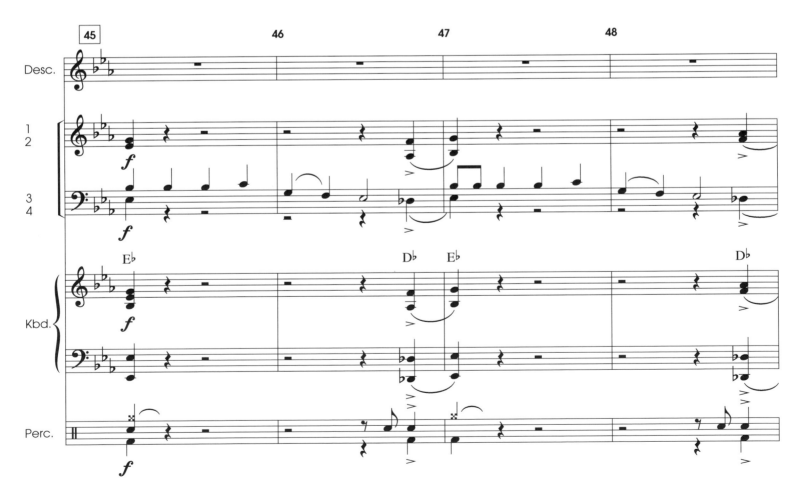

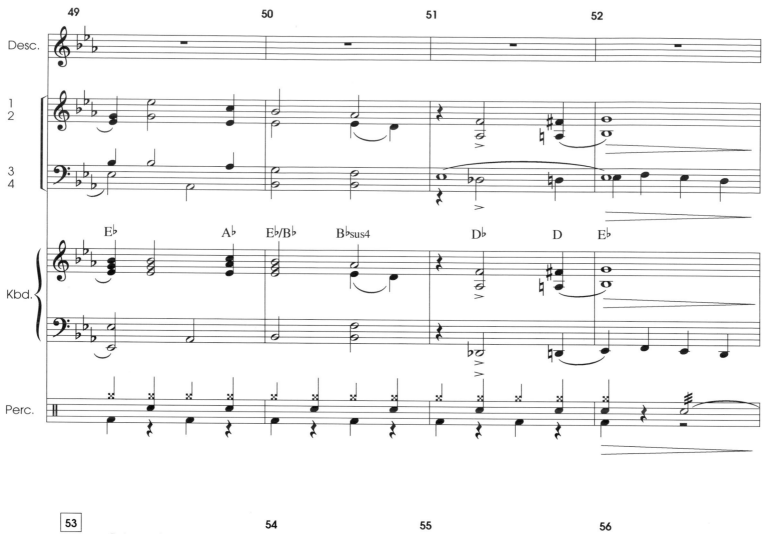

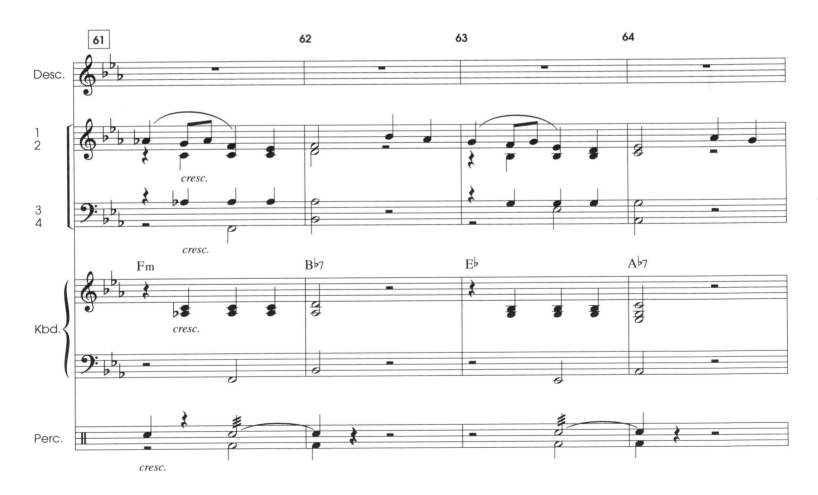

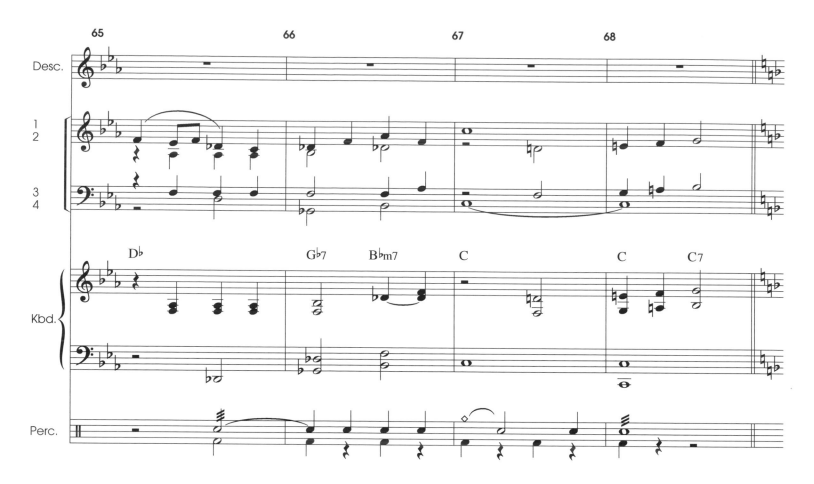

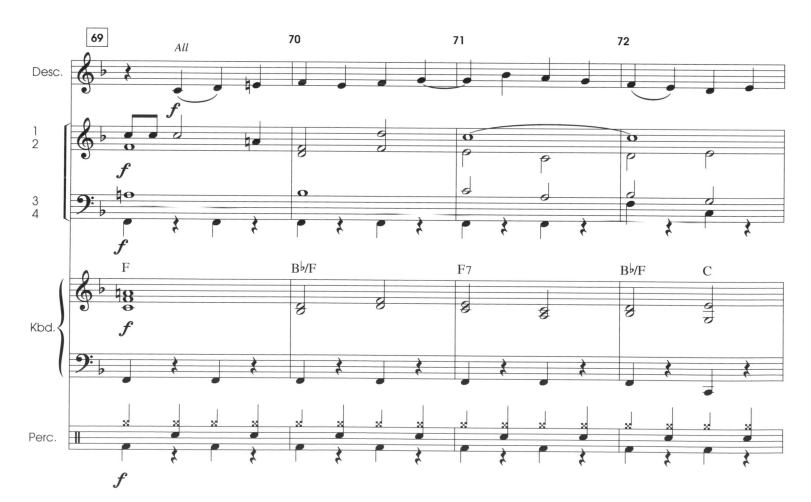

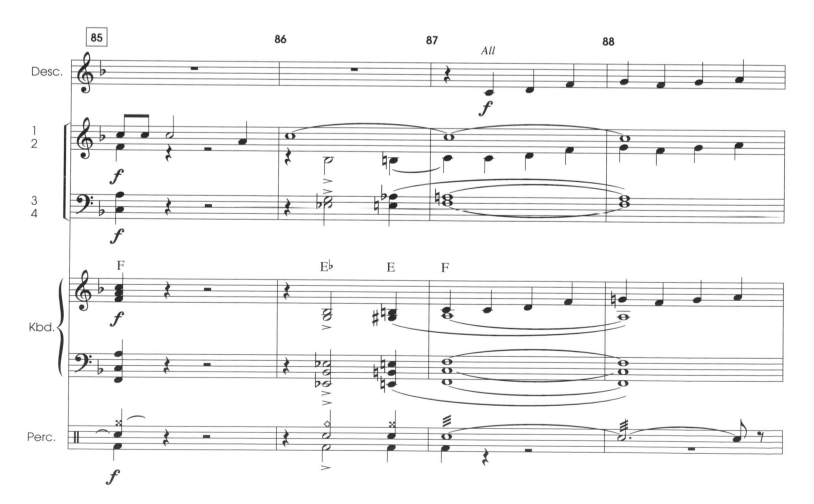

4. THIS IS MY FATHER'S WORLD

Duration: 2:15

Arr. **Timothy Johnson** (ASCAP)

Duration: 1:50

5. VISION QUEST

Be Thou My Vision

Arr. **Paul Curnow**(ASCAP)

* If no Triangle, use Snare stick on Suspended Cymbal crown.
** If 2 bongos are available, use instead of Tom Toms.
*** If Percussion is not available, begin in measure 5.

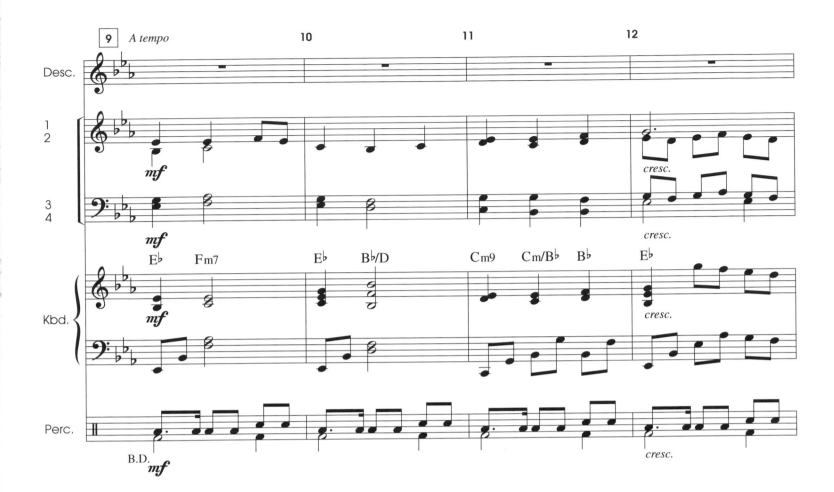

6. LORD, I WANT TO BE A CHRISTIAN

Arr. **Stephen Bulla** (ASCAP)

Duration: 2:15

7. ANGELS WE HAVE HEARD ON HIGH

Arr. **Stephen Bulla** (ASCAP)

8. O COME, O COME, EMMANUEL

Arr. **James Curnow** (ASCAP)

Duration: 3:00

+ If no Keyboard or Percussion is available, start here.
* Flugel Horn if available

57

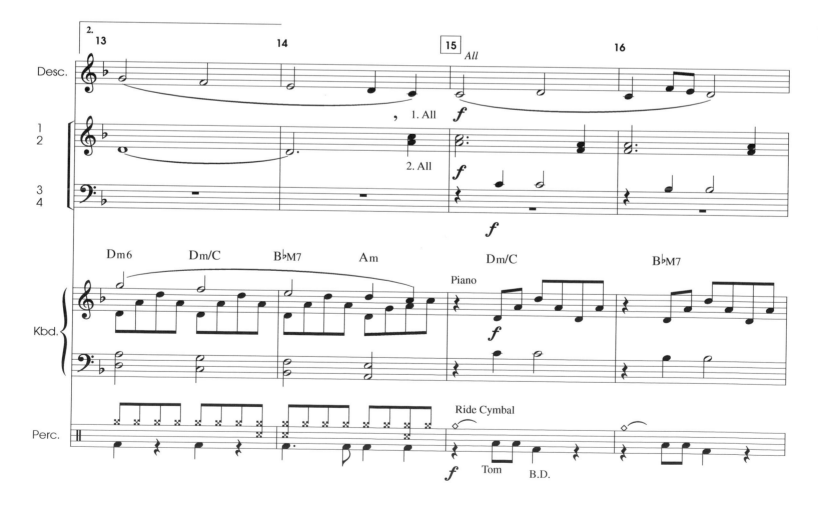

** Optional Flugel Horn to Trumpet

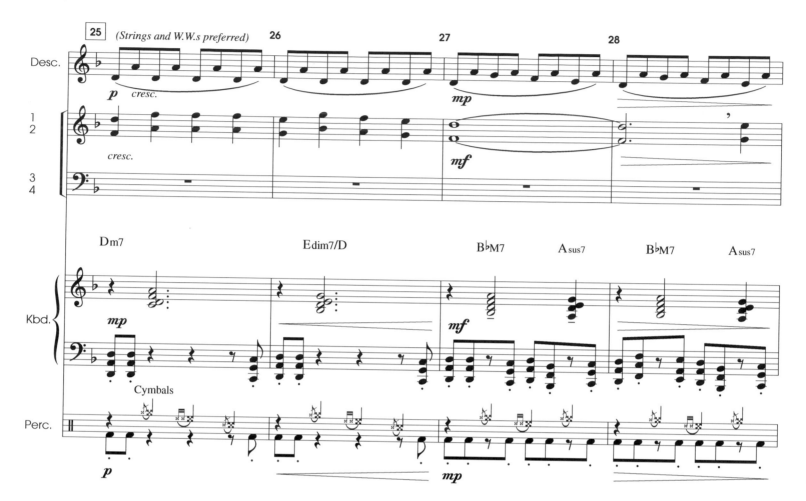

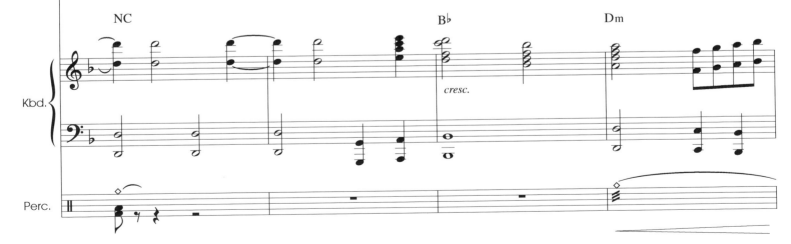

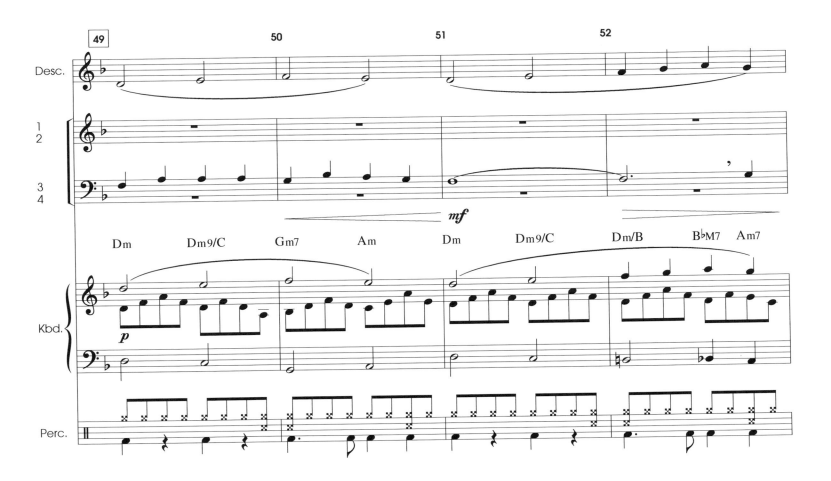

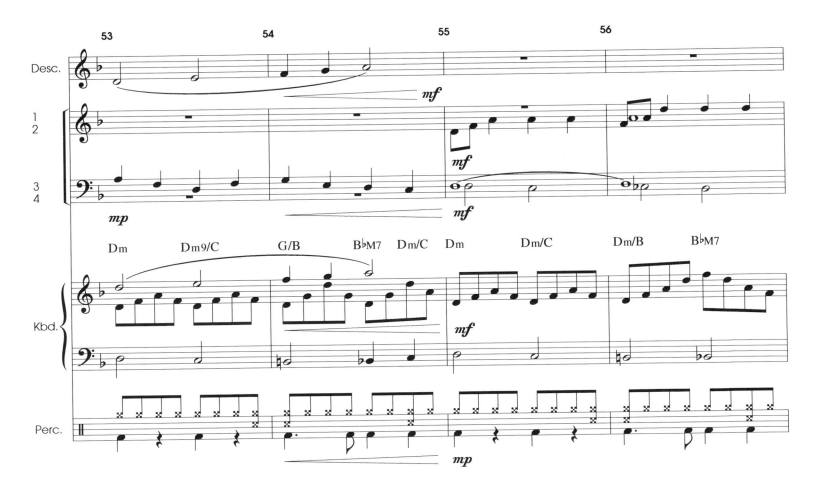

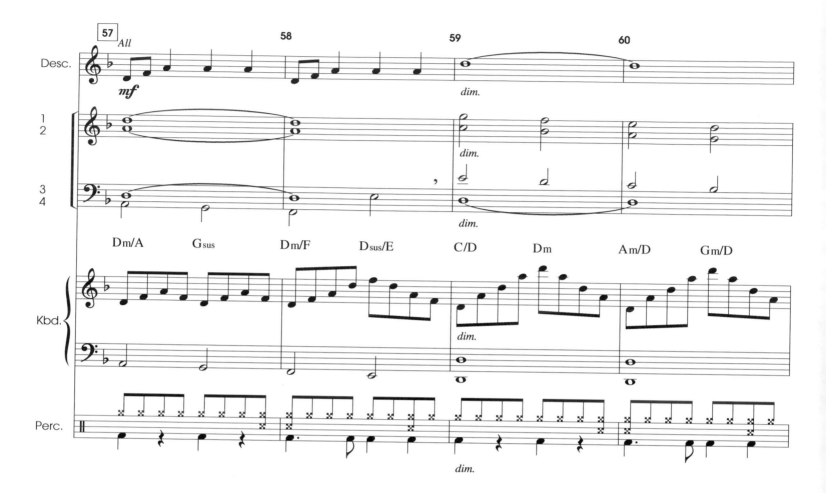

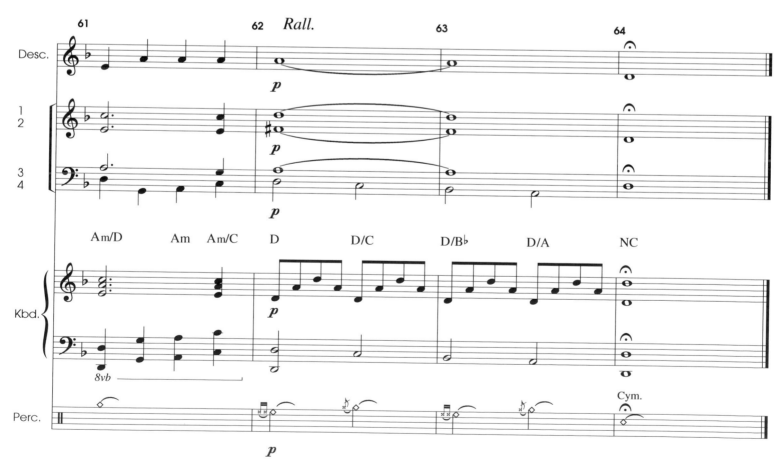

9. COVENTRY CAROL

Arr. **James Curnow**(ASCAP)

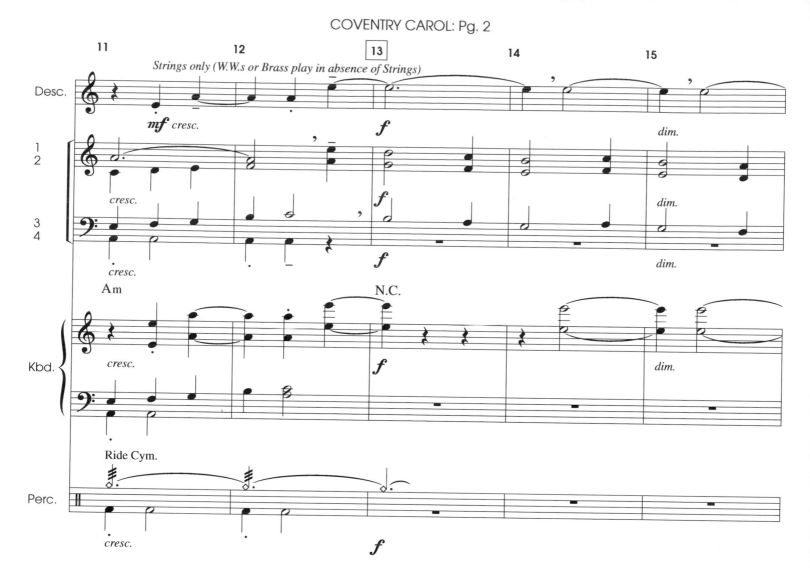

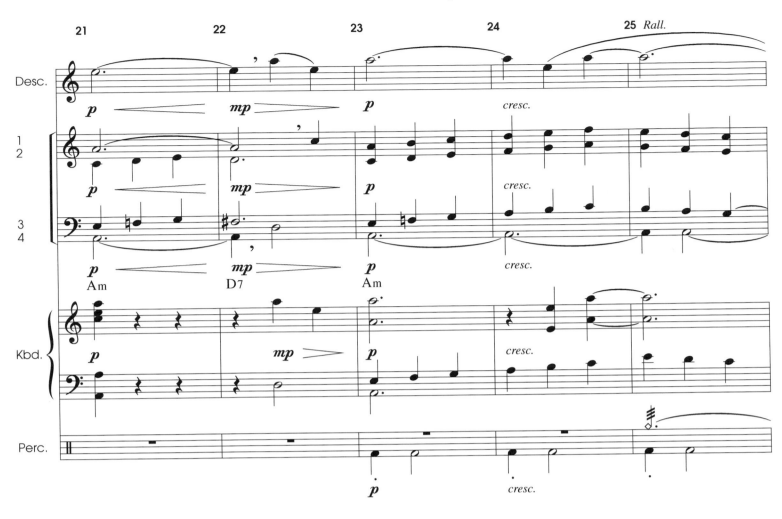

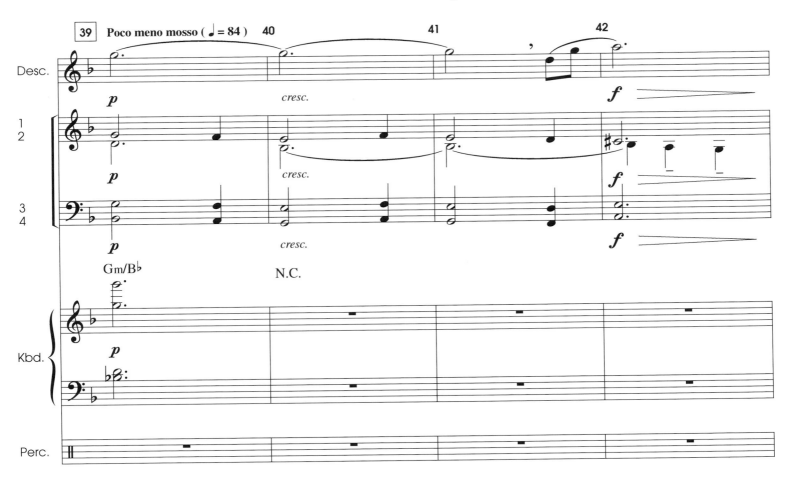

10. GOOD CHRISTIAN MEN, REJOICE

Arr. **James Curnow**(ASCAP)

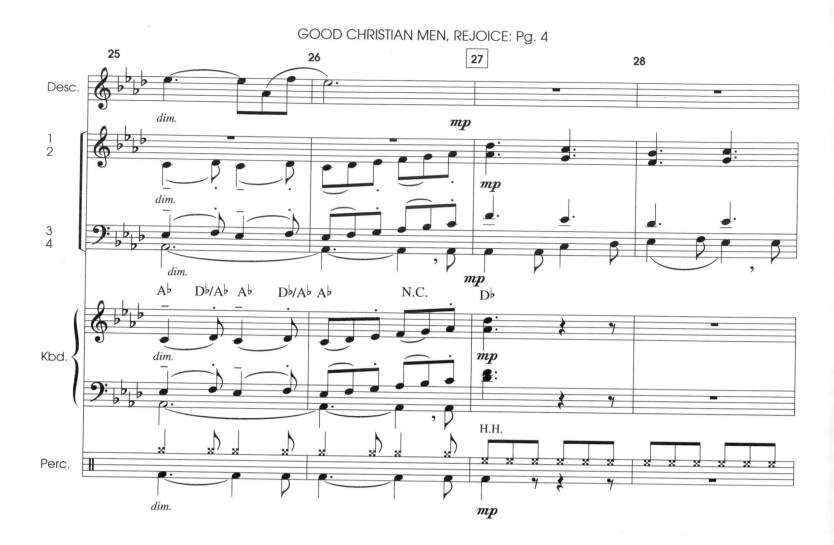

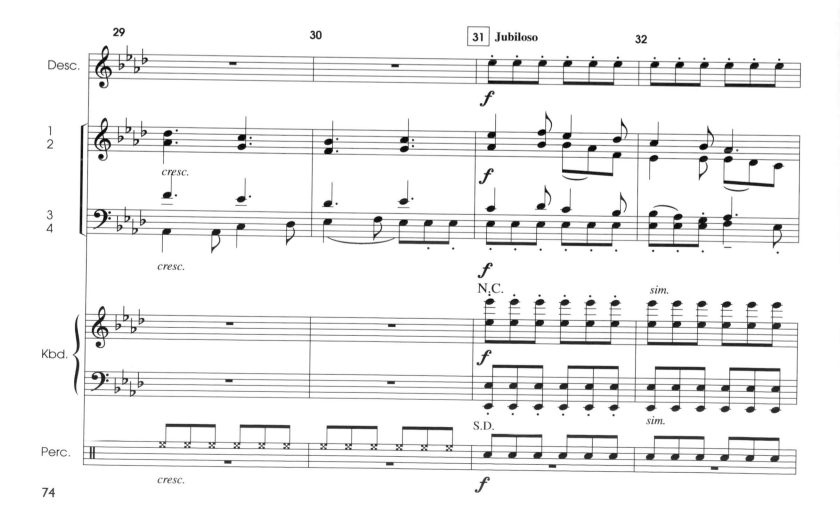

74

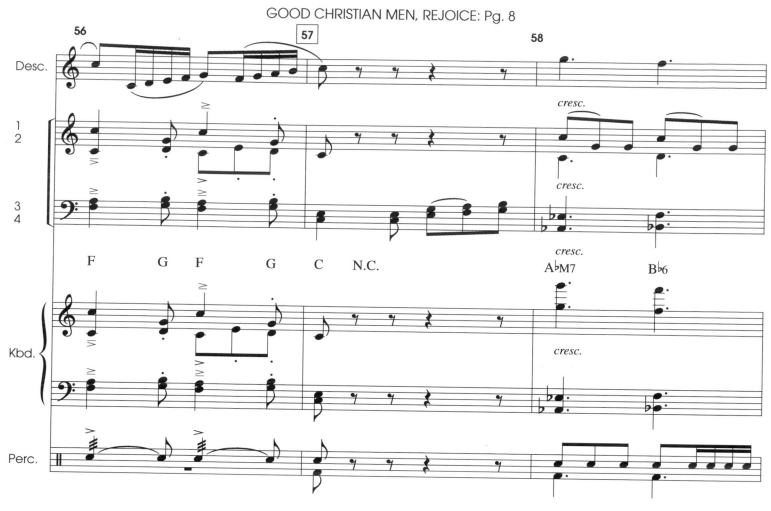

Also Available

A CHRISTMAS CELEBRATION *by James Curnow*

A CHRISTMAS CELEBRATION is a collection of sacred carols (arranged in 4 parts plus optional 5th part [descant]) designed to be used by just about every instrumental ensemble imaginable, including quartets and quintets of mixed instruments, to full orchestras, wind bands, or brass bands.

CHRISTMAS: SHORT AND SUITE *by William Himes*

These twelve Christmas favorites, orchestrated in 6-part flexible arrangements, will be a valuable asset to every church's music library. Including pieces from grade 2 through 4 makes CHRISTMAS: SHORT AND SUITE useful with a wide range of musicians. You may choose to program some of the pieces with full band, and others with small ensembles. The options are unlimited!

CMP PRAISE AND ADORATION SERIES

This series of concert band arrangements of sacred tunes are designed for use in either sacred or secular settings. They are graded according to standard concert band guidelines, and are orchestrated according to those guidelines.

A Hanover Prelude	Paul Curnow	Grade 2	CMP 0074.96
A Little Suite Praise	Paul Curnow	Grade 2	CMP 0490.01
Be Thou My Vision	Bryan Kidd	Grade 2	CMP 0229.98
Faith Triumphant	Douglas Court	Grade 2	CMP 0431.00
Fanfare and Canticle	Paul Curnow	Grade 2	CMP 0123.97
Feel the Spirit	Timothy Johnson	Grade 2	CMP 0316.99
O For A Thousand Tongues	Douglas Court	Grade 2	CMP 0188.98
All Creatures of Our God	Stephen Bulla	Grade 3	CMP 0106.96
Jericho	arr. William Himes	Grade 3	CMP 0017.95
Let It Shine!	James L. Hosay	Grade 3	CMP 0131.97
Rhapsodic Trilogy	Paul Curnow	Grade 3	CMP 0037.95
Shipston Prelude	Stephen Bulla	Grade 3	CMP 0499.00
The Valiant	Douglas Court	Grade 3	CMP 0253.99
Voluntary on Old 100th	arr. James Curnow	Grade 3	CMP 0507.01
All Hail the Power	Stephen Bulla	Grade 4	CMP 0122.97
Doxology	arr. William Himes	Grade 4	CMP 0019.95
Fanfare Prelude "And Can It Be?"	Timothy Johnson	Grade 4	CMP 0457.00
Fanfare Prelude "O God Our Help In Ages Past"	James Curnow	Grade 4	CMP 0258.99
Fanfare Prelude on the Hymn "Italian Hymn"	James Curnow	Grade 4	CMP 0043.95
Prelude on a Hymn of Praise	James Curnow	Grade 4	CMP 0080.96

GREAT HYMNS *arr. by James Curnow*

The inspiring sounds of 10 best-loved hymns are yours for the playing in James Curnow's GREAT HYMNS book with CD accompaniment. Songs included are: ALL CREATURES OF OUR GOD AND KING; PRAISE TO THE LORD, THE ALMIGHTY; BE THOU MY VISION; O WORSHIP THE KING; JOYFUL, JOYFUL, WE ARE THEE; BRETHREN, WE HAVE MET TO WORSHIP; WE GATHER TOGETHER; I SING THE MIGHTY POWER OF GOD; A MIGHTY FORTRESS IS OUR GOD; ALL HAIL THE POWER.
The Bb book is the first of our new Philip Smith series – the demonstration CD is performed by Philip Smith, Principal Trumpet with the New York Philharmonic. You won't want to miss it!
These sacred hymns are an important part of our rich sacred heritage and, as such, are appropriate for almost any venue.
Books are available for the following instruments: Flute, Oboe, Violin, Clarinet, Alto Saxophone, Tenor Saxophone, Trumpet, Euphonium (B.C. and T.C.), Horn, Trombone, and Piano Accompaniment.

TWO FOR CHRISTMAS *arr. by James Curnow*   *Instrumental Duets for Christmas*

Available for C, Bb, Eb, F, and Bass Clef instruments, these simple unaccompanied duets will be useful year after year. They can be played by two instruments of the same type, or any combination of the instruments listed above.
These familiar carols, including great melodies such as JOY TO THE WORLD, COVENTRY CAROL, ANGELS WE HAVE HEARD ON HIGH, and many more, will be welcomed anywhere Christmas is being celebrated.

CHRISTMAS JOY *arr. by Stephen Bulla*   *Instrumental Solos for Christmas*

Stephen Bulla has assembled a great collection of Grade 3 (Medium) Christmas solos which can be performed either with the included CD or with piano accompaniment. The included CD can be used in performance or as a wonderful practice tool. It allows solo musicians to perform recitals of their own for families and friends, at school, in church, or with a portable CD player, just about any place you can imagine. Books available are: Flute, Clarinet, Alto Saxophone, Trumpet, Trombone, Euphonium (B.C. and T.C.) and Piano Accompaniment.

GLORIA! *arr. by Stephen Bulla*   *Instrumental Solos for Easter*

This collection of familiar hymns has been chosen to be particularly appropriate for the Easter season.
The solos are arranged in a straightforward style, although frequent obligato and variation passages are interwoven with the familiar melodies to add interest. The ranges of difficulty are moderate, with the hope that the settings will provide something for everyone from novice to professional player. Books available are: Flute, Clarinet, Alto Saxophone, Trumpet, Trombone, Euphonium (T.C. and B.C.) and Piano Accompaniment.

THE SPLENDOR OF CHRISTMAS

This series of concert band arrangements of Christmas tunes is designed for use in either sacred or secular settings. They are graded according to standard concert band guidelines, and are orchestrated according to those guidelines.

Christmas Lullaby	Douglas Court	Grade 1	CMP 0409.00
Good King Wenceslas	Stephen Bulla	Grade 1	CMP 0147.97
Jolly Old Sleigh Ride	James Curnow	Grade 1	CMP 0073.96
Joyful and Triumphant	Douglas Court	Grade 1	CMP 0306.99
The Festive Season	Paul Curnow	Grade 1	CMP 0204.98
We Wish You a Merry Christmas	Elliot Del Borgo	Grade 1	CMP 0206.98
A Christmas Proclamation	Douglas Court	Grade 1½	CMP 0187.98
A Coventry Christmas	Paul Curnow	Grade 1½	CMP 0052.95
Variations on a French Carol	James Curnow	Grade 1½	CMP 0072.96
We Three Kings	James L. Hosay	Grade 1½	CMP 0168.97
Wintermusic	Paul Curnow	Grade 1½	CMP 0310.99
A Christmas Trilogy	Elliot Del Borgo	Grade 2	CMP 0139.97
A Sleigh Ride Fantasy	Timothy Johnson	Grade 2	CMP 0209.98
Allegria! Allegria! Allegria!	Stephen Bulla	Grade 2	CMP 0178.98
Christmas in Jamaica	Mike Hannickel	Grade 2	CMP 0250.99
English Carol Fantasy	James Curnow	Grade 2	CMP 0489.01
For Unto Us	George F. Handel, arranged by James Curnow	Grade 2	CMP 0130.97
International Christmas Salute	James Curnow	Grade 2	CMP 0101.96
Night of Wonder	Douglas Court	Grade 2	CMP 0488.01
O Little Town	arranged by Alfred Reed	Grade 2	CMP 0011.95
O Most Wonderful	arranged by Alfred Reed	Grade 2	CMP 0075.96
The Carolers	James Curnow	Grade 2	CMP 0129.97
Russian Carol Variations	Stephen Bulla	Grade 2	CMP 0318.99
With Sweet Jubilation	James Curnow	Grade 2	CMP 0429.00
A Holly Jolly Holiday	Stephen Bulla	Grade 2½	CMP 0496.01
Holly Variations	Mike Hannickel	Grade 2½	CMP 0438.00
A Christmas Celebration	James Curnow	Grade 2-3-4	CMP 0195.98
A Celtic Christmas	James L. Hosay	Grade 3	CMP 0504.01
A Christmas Collage	Douglas Court	Grade 3	CMP 0090.96
A Christmas Flourish	James Curnow	Grade 3	CMP 0198.98
Bethlehem Triptych	Stephen Bulla	Grade 3	CMP 0181.98
Christmas Adoration	Paul Curnow	Grade 3	CMP 0157.97
Christmas Calypso	Stephen Bulla	Grade 3	CMP 0167.97
Christmas Carillon	James Curnow	Grade 3	CMP 0256.99
Christmas in Europe	Timothy Johnson	Grade 3	CMP 0447.00
Christmas Party	James Curnow	Grade 3	CMP 0505.01
I Wonder as I Wander	James L. Hosay	Grade 3	CMP 0446.00
Joy to the World	arranged by Paul Curnow	Grade 3	CMP 0018.95
Sweet Little Jesus Boy	James L. Hosay	Grade 3	CMP 0254.99
Christmas Fancies	James Curnow	Grade 4	CMP 0456.00
Overture to a Winter Festival	James Curnow	Grade 4	CMP 0042.95
The Bells of Christmas	Stephen Bulla	Grade 4	CMP 0323.99
Westminster Carol	James L. Hosay	Grade 4	CMP 0070.96